I Still Believe in Unicorns

by
Bob Stanish

Cover by Vanessa Filkins

Copyright © Good Apple, 1992

ISBN No. 0-86653-674-4

Printing No. 987654321

Good Apple
1204 Buchanan St., Box 299
Carthage, IL 62321-0299

S I M O N & S C H U S T E R *A Paramount Communications Company*

Acknowledgements

To

Troy Cole, Educational consultant and writer,
Edwardsville, Illinois

for the foreword

and to

Mary H. Fisher, Coordinator of the Academically Gifted,
Guilford County School System,
Greensboro, North Carolina

Sylvia Lewis, State Consultant of Academically Gifted Programs,
North Carolina State Department of Public Education,
Raleigh, North Carolina

Cynthia M. Dagnal-Myron of the African-American Studies Department,
Tucson Unified School District,
Tucson, Arizona

Jo Ann Sellers of the GATE/PLUS Program,
Tucson Unified School District,
Tucson, Arizona

Virginia R. Troutman, Principal, Lewis Primary School
Carbondale Elementary School District,
Carbondale, Illinois

for their reviews of the manuscript.

GA1404

Table of Contents

GA1404

Foreword

Bob,

From *I Believe in Unicorns* to *I Still Believe in Unicorns*, your mindanderings have allowed us to share in your untiring search for mythical creatures.

Throughout your travels you have endeavored to preserve the unicorn and extend its domain. Unicorns, once endangered, now dwell in the hearts of those who believe. They have timidly ventured from the misty mountains and dewy dells to visit our minds.

Thank you, Bob, for your commitment to save the unicorn. We who know you will never let unicorns become extinct.

> Some still see unicorns
> though others may not
> but when you believe
> all it takes is a thought.

Troy and Betty Cole

GA1404

𝕴 Still Believe in Unicorns...

because imagination stimulates thinking

... into the *what if's,*
the *why not's*
and
the *what can be's.*

And through this:

... ideas and choices can multiply
... understandings and potentials are extended
... and dreams can become.

The thinking processes accommodated in this book are for this. They are not the processes for memorizing content but the processes for creating content. They can, with love, carry over into all realms of learning, doing and becoming.

As in 1979, with the publication of *I Believe in Unicorns*, I still believe in them and always will.

GA1404

What This Book Is About

INTRODUCTION PAGES contain an overview for nurturing and developing creative thinking in a classroom.

STUDENT PAGES will elicit one or more of the creative thinking skills cited in this book. These pages can be duplicated and used by individual students or in a teacher-directed setting involving a small group or the entire class. There is no specific sequence for the pages.

A TEACHER PAGE accompanies each student page. Each teacher page is formatted in the following way:

CREATIVE THINKING SKILLS... The focus will be on one or more of the six factors of creative thinking.

GETTING STARTED... A few guidelines for beginning the activity

AFTERWARDS... Suggestions on what to look for and possible extensions on the activity

MORE... Suggestions for broadening the idea or concept

GA1404

Processes Involved in Generating and Enhancing Ideas

Fluency...   Producing ideas in quantity

Flexibility...   Producing ideas that represent many categories of thought, different perspectives of viewing and alternative possibilities of doing

Elaboration...   Elaborating and embellishing on ideas in semantic, symbolic or figurative ways; adding to, explaining or enriching with detail

Originality...   Generating unique, novel or unusual ideas

Transformations...   Formulating new ideas through the transformations or modifications of existing ideas

Visualization...   Producing or responding to visual images that become ideas; enhancing ideas through visual imagery

The above processes, in varying combinations and clusters, stimulate and produce creative thought. Creative thinking is defined in this book by the above processes that accommodate and nurture it.

On Nurturing Creative Talent

Teacher Questioning

Your classroom questions can be frightening or exciting, intimidating or stimulating, expanding or restricting. It's not so much what is asked, but how it's asked.
- Ask more open-ended questions.
- Ask fewer "why" questions.

Responding to Student Responses

Be accepting to all student responses. Your response to their response is important! Create a climate where intellectual risk-taking is encouraged. Wait until an appropriate later time for assessing student responses. Never, never do this during a period of freewheeling thought or during brainstorming.

Varying the Techniques of Brainstorming

There are many, many techniques of brainstorming and brainwriting today! Find them and use them, for in doing so you facilitate in the development of intellectual talent. Techniques for generating ideas are lifelong things and not just classroom things.

Encourage Student Adaptations on What Is Learned

Challenge students to find ways to adapt what they learn in new and variant ways. "In what other ways might we use it?"

Structure Assignments with Limitations and Conditions

Structure, whenever possible, assigned problems and tasks with specified limitations and contingencies. Don't say, "Write an essay on the Civil War." Do say, "Make an imaginary entry into a diary of a Southern soldier a day before the Battle of Gettysburg. Include in this entry his thoughts, feelings and fears; quotes made to him by his comrades; and what he sees in the Union lines." Don't say, "Give us a definition of sliding friction." Do say, "Use a glass of water, a newspaper and a table to demonstrate what sliding friction is."

Nurture Inventiveness Through Structured Problem Solving

Make inventiveness an element of what is taught; for example, "Use a plastic sandwich bag, a small piece of masking tape, a paper drinking straw, a piece of construction paper and water to construct a reading glass for Cyclops." Then make the connection to subject matter; for example, "What purposes did the Greek Titans like Cyclops serve in Greek society?" or "What are the attributes of water and in what ways are they used? In what other ways might they be used?"

Display Unique Student Products Throughout the School

Encourage unique student products by acknowledging them with schoolwide displays and posted photographs. Acknowledge what is original and unique.

GA1404

Use an Array of Instructional Strategies That Facilitate the Skills of Problem Solving and Idea Generation.

- analogies and synectics-based techniques
- attribute listing
- brainstorming and webbing techniques
- force fit or forced relationships
- idea checklist or modification techniques
- inquiry or inductive methods
- morphological synthesis
- structured problem-solving methods

Use and Encourage Idea Assessment Through Criterion

Teach students how to use criterion in assessing ideas. Create posters of criteria items for ongoing classroom reference and use. Make available evaluation grids that make provisions for criteria and ideas or potential solutions.

Balance Classroom Activities into Realms of Preferences

- verbally spoken
- verbally written
- kinesthetic
- visual
- auditory

GA1404

Reduce Teacher Talk and Increase Student Interaction and Activity Through
- the use of clarifying responses for helping students analyze, synthesize and evaluate their thinking

    "Explain this in another way."

    "Are there other possibilities? Alternatives?"

    "How might this be paraphrased?"

    "What might happen if …?"

    "Can you give us some examples?"

    "What are the consequences?"

    "What factors led you to this understanding?"

    "Can you elaborate a little more?"

- the formulation of interactive groups for purposes of

    …cooperative learning

    …peer tutoring

    …problem-solving tasks

    …committee projects

    …peer editing

    …reactions and feedback on tasks and assignments

- student initiative and self-direction with

    …individual research, investigation and independent study

    …contractual learning arrangements

    …projects, data collection, experiments and inventions

GA1404

Enhancing Creative Potential Through Questioning and Strategy

To develop **fluency** in students, ask questions like
    "How many ways…?"
    "In what ways…?"
    "How might we…?"

Create strategies that
    encourage divergent thought and production
    stimulate multiple responses and possibilities
    stimulate additional inquiry and investigation

To develop **flexibility** in students, ask questions like
    "What other ways do you know to do this?"
    "What other ways could you view this?"
    "What are some different approaches?"
    "What are the different possibilities?"

Create strategies that
    require varying points of view
    encourage different perspectives and openness to other possibilities

To develop **elaboration** in students, ask questions like
    "In what ways might we enhance it?"
    "What else is needed?"
    "What details can be added?"
    "How might this be explained?"

Create strategies that require student effort to supplement, to enhance, to embellish, to improve and to explain.

? ? ? ? ? ?
? ? ? ? ?

GA1404

To develop **originality** in students, offer statements like
"Think of unusual or unique approaches to this problem!"
"Think far out!"
"Think of some novel possibilities!"

Create strategies that encourage student experimentation, manipulation and inventiveness.

To develop **transformations**, that is, the abilities to transform, provide and encourage the use of modification techniques and idea stimulation devices such as Bob Eberle's **SCAMPER**:

"What might be **s**ubstituted?"
"What might be **c**ombined?"
"What might be **a**dapted?"
"What might be **m**odified? **M**agnetized? **M**iniaturized?"
"What might be **p**ut to a different use?"
"What might be **e**liminated?"
"What might be **r**earranged? **R**eversed?"

Create strategies that are *intellectual building blocks*, strategies that require and encourage alteration and modification.

To develop **visualization,** give students these instructions:
"Describe what you think is there!"
"Describe what you can't see!"
"Describe what will happen next!"
"Sketch your idea!"

Create strategies that challenge students to describe or graphically illustrate what isn't immediately seen.

? ? ? ? ? ?

GA1404

On Connecting Creativity with Content

Through the Skills of Creative Thinking

There are many ways of doing this and here are a few simple examples.

Fluency
<u>List all</u> the questions <u>you</u> <u>can</u> <u>think</u> <u>of</u> in which the answer is *a short story*.

Flexibility
How many <u>different</u> things contain a spiral? Afterwards, *categorize* your responses into topic categories.

Elaboration
Write a different ending to Hemingway's *The Old Man and the Sea*. <u>Explain in detail</u> why you changed the ending.

Originality
<u>Create an original</u> collage with materials not normally found in a collage.

Transformations
What geographical <u>changes</u> on the subcontinent of India would you make to alter and increase food production?

Visualization
<u>Visualize</u> the kinds of visual images that might have entered Einstein's mind while he was processing his formula of $E = MC^2$.

The underlined word or words within the content statements are the stimulators for programming the type of creative thinking desired.

$$E=MC^2$$

GA1404

Through Creative Strategy or Activity

There are many ways of integrating creative strategies with subject matter.

Analogies
- In what ways is magnetism like a sweater?
- What would it be like to be a positive electrical charge? Describe how you would function and how you would depend on other things and conditions.

Attribute Listing
- List the attributes of a square. Which of these attributes would apply to other shapes and forms?
- List the attributes of a sponge. Use a few of these words in developing a characterization of a fictional story character.

Brainstorming
- In what ways might we demonstrate, in experiments, the principle of Bernoulli? Which of these ways would be the most cost effective? The safest? The most dynamic?

Forced Relationships
or
Forced Associations
or
Force Fit
- Force a fit between some nouns and verbs for some unique gerunds.
- Force a fit between two antonyms for an interesting story title reflecting conflict, for example, "Deafening Silence!"

MAGNETISM

GA1404

Idea Checklists
(Modification
Techniques)

Encourage students to use a checklist on all projects, written work and assigned activities when applicable. Checklists stimulate ideas. Here are some examples.

- What could be substituted to improve this?
- What could be combined to improve this?
- What could be adapted to improve this?
- What could be altered to improve this?
- What could be modified to improve this?
- What could be emphasized or de-emphasized to improve this?
- What could be rearranged to improve this?
- What could be reduced to improve this?
- What could be eliminated to improve this?
- What could be added to improve this?
- What could be reversed to improve this?

Inquiry or Inductive Strategies

There are a variety of ways to structure activities to promote curiosity, data collection, hypothesizing and theorizing. The use of the following kinds of problems are excellent for stimulating inquiry:

- problems involving paradoxes
- problems involving ambiguities
- problems involving discrepant events

? ? ? ? ? ?

GA1404

Morphological Synthesis　　This is an excellent strategy for developing

- story writing themes and plots
- poetry which is highly structured such as cinquain, haiku, tanka, etc.
- invention ideas
- unique book report or presentation ideas

Structured Problem Solving

Structured problem-solving methods and processes appropriate for content and curriculum inclusion and integration can be found within a variety of titles, programs and materials. The most highly recommended are the following:

- Creative Problem Solving (CPS)
- Future Problem-Solving Materials
- Synectics Techniques
- Odyssey of the Mind Problems
- Materials made available through the U.S. Patent and Trademark Office, PROJECT XL and The National Inventive Thinking Association (NITA)

Sources and Notes

For additional information on morphological synthesis, attribute listing, forced relationships and other strategies:

Davis, Gary A. *Creativity Is Forever*, 2nd edition. Dubuque, Iowa: Kendall/Hunt Publishing Company, 1986.

For the originating source of SCAMPER:

Eberle, Robert F. *Scamper: Games for Imagination Development*. Buffalo, New York: D.O.K. Publishers, Inc., 1971.

For information on synectics and analogies:

Gordon, W.J.J. *Synectics*. New York: Harper & Row, 1961.

On transformations:

Guilford, J.P., *Way Beyond the I.Q.* Buffalo, New York: The Creative Education Foundation, 1977.

For information on creative problem solving and idea assessment through criterion:

Isaksen, Scott G., and Donald J. Treffinger. *Creative Problem Solving: The Basic Course*. Buffalo, New York: Bearly Limited, 1985.

For information on teacher questioning techniques:

Johnson, Nancy L. *Questioning Makes the Difference*. Dayton, Ohio: Creative Learning Consultants, 1990.

Information on preferences:

McCarthy, Bernice. *The 4Mat System: Teaching to Learning Styles with Right/Left Mode Techniques*. Barrington, Illinois: Excel, Inc., 1987.

GA1404

On visualization:

McKim, Robert H. *Thinking Visually: A Strategy Manual for Problem Solving*. Belmont, California: Wadsworth, 1980.

On the clarifying response:

Raths, Louis E., Merrill Harmin, and Sidney B. Simon. *Values and Teaching*. rev. ed. Columbus, Ohio: Charles E. Merrill Publishing Co., 1977.

On references made to *I Believe in Unicorns*:

Stanish, Bob. *I Believe in Unicorns*. Carthage, Illinois: Good Apple, Inc., 1977.

On classroom inventions and inventiveness:

Stanish, Bob, and Carol Singletary. *Inventioneering*. Carthage, Illinois: Good Apple, Inc., 1987.

Fluency, flexibility, elaboration and originality as measurable factors of creative thinking:

Torrance, E. Paul. *The Torrance Tests of Creative Thinking. Norms Technical Manual*. Lexington, Massachusetts: Personnel Press/Ginn, 1966.

For information on varied techniques of brainstorming and brainwriting:

Van Gundy, Arthur B., Jr. *Techniques of Structured Problem Solving*. New York: Van Nostrand Reinhold Company, 1981.

Note: A few illustrations in this book were originally created for *I Believe in Unicorns* by Nancee Volpe McClure. These illustrations can be found on pages 2, 13, 48 and 92. The illustration on page 30 was done "in house" by the Good Apple Art Department.

GA1404

What Kinds of Chores Would You Give a Fire-Breathing Dragon?

<u>Relight the pilot light on the furnace</u>.

_____

_____

_____

_____

_____

_____

_____

_____

_____

_____

_____

_____

_____

_____

_____

_____

_____

_____

_____

GA1404

What Kinds of Chores Would You Give a Fire-Breathing Dragon?

Creative Thinking Skill   Fluency

Getting Started   Fluency deals with the generation of many ideas and the concept of fire should generate several, for example, burning leaves, trash, roasting marshmallows, warming up a pizza, clearing and melting snow from a driveway, etc. Motivation to generate ideas is in the encouragement and acceptance of all ideas.

This exercise can be done individually or in teams of two or three students.

Afterwards   Consider some of these options:
1. Write a story about a dragon who stayed a week at your house.
2. Speculate how and why dragons entered the minds of men.
3. Name some famous stories that have dragons in them.
4. How many different words can be written using the letters in the word *dragon*?
5. Write some alliteration sentences using the word *dragon*; for example, *Danny Dragon drives downhill disastrously*.

Unicorns place a high value on all living things.

GA1404

Dress Up a Funny Looking Elephant in a Funny Way!

Think about it!
Make the clothes colorful and outlandish!
Laugh about it!
Make up a story about it!
Share the clothes and the story!

18

GA1404

Dress Up a Funny Looking Elephant in a Funny Way!

Creative Thinking Skill

Elaboration

Elaboration is the embellishment of a concept. Look for a variety of clothing additions to the elephant.

Getting Started

Encourage students to decorate the elephant in a creative way. Colorings and drawings that represent patterns, textures and decorations are an effective way of doing this.

Afterwards

Encourage students to share and describe their creations.

More

Provide time for written stories about the elephant who became a circus clown.

Unicorns care!

List Different Ways to Determine the Time Without Looking at a Watch or Clock or Asking, "What's the Time?"

_____   _____

_____   _____

Buy a TV schedule!_____   _____

_____   _____

_____   _____

_____   _____

_____   _____

_____   _____

_____   _____

_____   _____

_____   _____

_____   _____

GA1404

List Different Ways to Determine the Time Without Looking at a Watch or Clock or Asking, "What's the Time?"

Creative Thinking Skills

Flexibility and fluency

Flexibility deals with different categories of thought. For instance all responses related to written schedules could be categorized as a category of thought dealing with written schedules; all responses related to personal habits and time frames could be categorized together; all responses related to the sun and shadows could be categorized together; all responses dealing with sound, for example, bells, whistles, alarms, could be categorized together; all responses dealing with mechanized routines, for example, trains, buses, streetlights turned on at a certain time, etc., could be classified together. To determine flexibility, determine how many different categories of thought are represented in student responses. The more categories listed, the higher the flexibility. Flexibility deals with viewing a problem from a variety of perspectives and points of view. Flexibility is a very important factor in creative thinking.

Getting Started

1. Distribute copies of the activities to all students and provide them a time frame of ten minutes to do the exercise.

2. Involve students in creating categories and have them categorize their responses accordingly.

Afterwards

Discuss the importance of viewing a problem from many different perspectives, angles and points of view.

GA1404

What's Inside?

Think about it!
Allow your mind to see it!
Draw a "looking down at it" picture!
Talk about how it works!

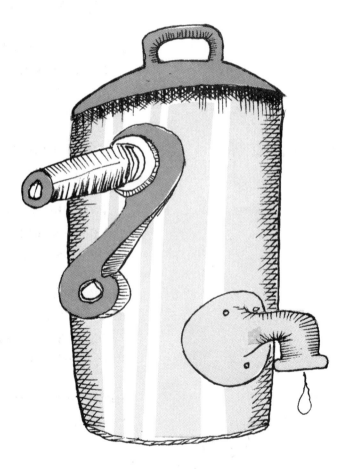

22

GA1404

What's Inside?

Creative Thinking Skills   Visualization

Visualization is the ability to stimulate, generate or enhance ideas in the mind's eye.

Getting Started

1. Distribute copies of the exercise to all students. With younger students have them imagine they are standing over the machine. Have them imagine the lid is removed from it. Encourage them to imagine the inside working parts of it.

2. Have them draw the inside parts and then share their drawings with two other classmates. After the sharing, encourage all students to make revisions, if desired, on their drawings.

Afterwards

1. Share and discuss the drawn images as a total class.

2. Discuss what kinds of things could be changed into a liquid by the machine. (How many different things could be used with the machine?)

3. As a class, categorize the responses into categories of thought (fruits, vegetables, nonedible items, etc.). Which category had the greater quantity of responses?

More   Encourage students to present a commercial on the machine.

   GA1404

Create a Robotic Grocery Shopping Cart from a Few Spare Parts

A is a large mechanical hand.
B is a piece of roof guttering with an elbow.
C is a suction plunger.
D is a garbage can.
E is a metal lamp shade.
F is a large water bucket.
G is a skateboard.

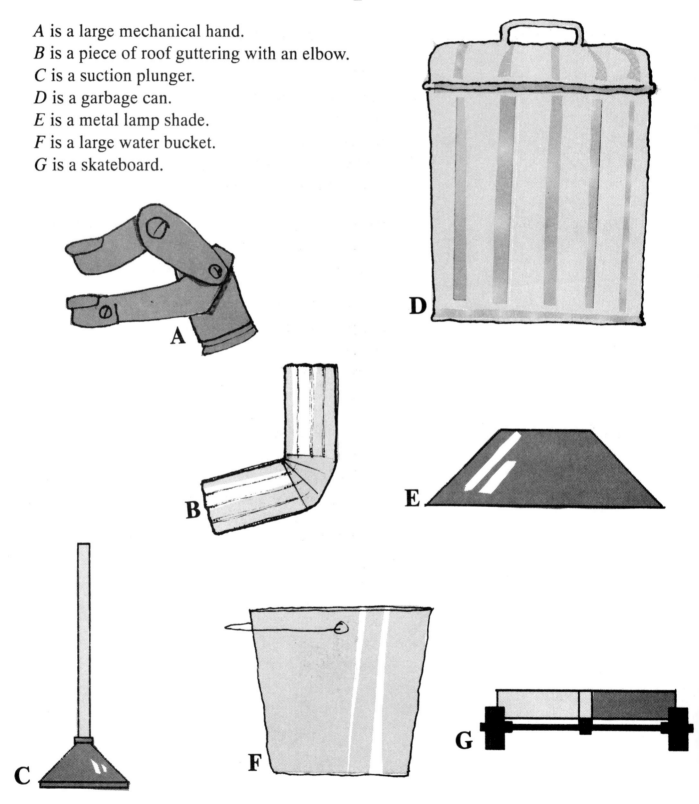

GA1404

Create a Robotic Grocery Shopping Cart from a Few Spare Parts

Creative Thinking Skills   Transformations and visualization

The transformations in this exercise would be causing concepts, in a symbolic and figurative sense, to serve different purposes. Transformations would also include substitution, rearrangement and combining different components into a synthesis. Visualization is required to complete the synthesis.

Getting Started

1. Distribute copies of the exercise page along with scissors, glue and white construction paper to students.

2. Instruct students to piece together a robotic shopping cart using all of the exercise parts. Encourage them to experiment with part locations before making a decision as to final placement before gluing.

Afterwards

1. Have students either tell or describe in writing how the shopping cart functions and the various benefits it provides. Ask students to explain what new functions their spare parts now have.

2. Provide time for sharing both constructions and stories.

GA1404

In What Ways Might You Get a Hibernating Grizzly Bear out of a Clothes Closet?

Blow a bugle!

_____

_____

_____

_____

Do some sound effects of summer.

_____

_____

_____

_____

_____

_____

_____

_____

_____

_____

_____

_____

_____

_____

_____

_____

_____

_____

_____

_____

26

GA1404

In What Ways Might You Get a Hibernating Grizzly Bear out of a Clothes Closet?

Creative Thinking Skills   Fluency and originality

Getting Started

This exercise deals with both fluency, originality and some of the beginning skills of group problem solving.

1. Place your class in groups of four students. If their writing skills are adequate, have them rotate one copy of the student activity sheet in which ideas are silently written on the paper by each student within the group. Have them follow these simple directions: "Write one idea on the paper then pass the paper to the person sitting on your right. The person receiving the paper writes one idea on the paper and then passes the paper to the person sitting on his or her right. In other words, as you receive the paper write an idea on it. Continue in this fashion until I tell you to stop. Do not talk during this exercise."

2. After seven or eight minutes, stop the exercise. Have each group determine how many written ideas they have (fluency). Have each group determine which written response (criterion) was...
   - the funniest
   - the least expensive
   - the safest
   - the most likely to succeed
   - the most original (the idea no other group would likely have)

If writing skills are not adequate, have a total group brainstorming session in which you list their ideas on the chalkboard, then follow the criterion suggestions cited above.

Afterwards

Discuss the importance of rating ideas on the basis of criterion, for example, expense, safety, likely to succeed, etc.

GA1404

5-Square Scramble

One, two, three and four-letter words are worth 1 point per letter.
Five-letter words are worth 10 points.
Six-letter words are worth 15 points.

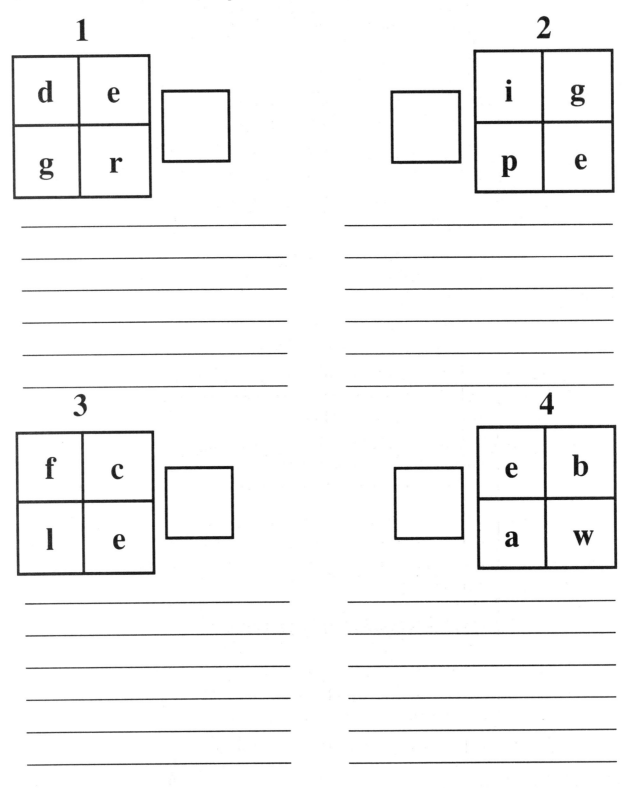

1

d	e
g	r

2

i	g
p	e

3

f	c
l	e

4

e	b
a	w

GA1404

5-Square Scramble

Rules

• Add any letter to each of the four groupings for a grid of five letters. Use the letters given plus one free choice letter to create words. Once the free choice letter is written in the box, it becomes a permanent letter.

• Any letter in each grouping may be used more than once.

• A letter or letters in each grouping may be eliminated to create words.

• See how many points can be made in each grouping. Proper names may not be used.

• All words formed may be challenged. If challenged, a dictionary must be used to justify the word or the spelling of the word.

• Points awarded:
  1-letter words are worth 1 point.
  2-letter words are worth 2 points.
  3-letter words are worth 3 points.
  4-letter words are worth 4 points.
  5-letter words are worth 10 points.
  6-letter words are worth 15 points.
  Misspelled words = 0 points.

Creative Thinking Skill   Fluency

Getting Started   Provide the rules of the game to all students. As an example, suppose the free letter choice in the first grouping is the letter *A*. Examples of words formed with the four letters plus the free choice letter *A* might include:

grade = 10 points	greed = 10 points
egg = 3 points	dread = 10 points
dear = 4 points	grad = 4 points
reader = 15 points	total = 56 points

wards   Acknowledge students who had high scores.

GA1404

GA1404

Building Houses and Homes

Materials Needed to Build Houses

nails _____

_____

_____

_____

_____

_____

_____

_____

_____

_____

_____

_____

_____

_____

_____

Materials Needed to Build Homes

love _____

_____

_____

_____

_____

_____

_____

_____

_____

_____

_____

_____

_____

_____

Building Houses and Homes

Creative Thinking Skill   Fluency

Getting Started   Place students in teams of two or three students to compile a list of materials for both houses and homes. Provide five to ten minutes for completion.

Afterwards

1. Ask: "Which list was more difficult to compile? Why do you suppose it's more difficult to build a home than a house?"

2. Encourage students to share some of their responses.

More   Use a few of these word concepts to extend the concept of "home building": caring, sensitivity to others, sharing, attending to the concerns of others, courtesy, a willingness to listen, tenderness, cherishing values, commitments met, effort, willingness to help, participating, contributing, love, resolving conflicts, trusting, giving, receiving, complimenting, coordinating, honesty, conscientiousness, consideration, dependability, feeling positive, being helpful, forthright, being friendly, learning, trying, supporting, praising, a sense of humor, doing things together, charitable, hope, respect, cooperating, pride, achieving, etc.

GA1404

Different Perspectives

Look at the picture from different angles and write what it could be.

_____

_____

_____

a smiling face _____

_____

_____

a snail

GA1404

Different Perspectives

Creative Thinking Skills   Flexibility, transformations and visualization

Getting Started

1. Have students list things the design could be from varying angles of viewing. Encourage them to turn their papers accordingly for listing purposes.

2. Although this exercise can be done individually, consider pairing students into teams of two's.

Afterwards

Share perspectives.

Role-play varying perspectives on a dolphin through the following cast of characters:
* a manager of a water show featuring dolphins
* a paying customer to the water show
* a researcher on dolphins
* a fisherman who sometimes, mistakenly, nets dolphins in his nets
* an ocean ecologist

More

List issues where there are multiple points of view.

GA1404

Draw in an Invention Idea That Would Help an Overweight Kangaroo Get Across a Busy City Street!

- Think about it!
- Draw it!
- Label the parts!
- Share it!
- Talk about it!
- Laugh about it!

34

Draw in an Invention Idea That Would Help an Overweight Kangaroo Get Across a Busy City Street!

Creative Thinking Skills

Flexibility, elaboration, originality, transformations and visualization

Getting Started

1. Begin by nurturing flexibility of thinking. For example, ask students to...

   • List things with wheels–*wheelchairs, skateboards, wagons, etc.*

   • List things that spring or bounce–*springs, balls, pogo sticks, etc.*

   • List things that would attract attention–*flashing lights, helium-filled balloons, etc.*

   • List things that create harsh sounds–*sirens, whistles, public address systems, etc.*

2. Challenge students to think about how some things listed might be combined into an invention to get the overweight kangaroo across the street.

3. Provide time and the exercise sheet to all students.

Afterwards

Share drawings, descriptions and laughter.

More

Discuss how the need for an invention stimulates the imagination to create it.

GA1404

The Creature

- Create your main character by assembling and gluing some body parts together on a piece of construction paper.

- Then write a story about the evil looking creature who couldn't be cruel.

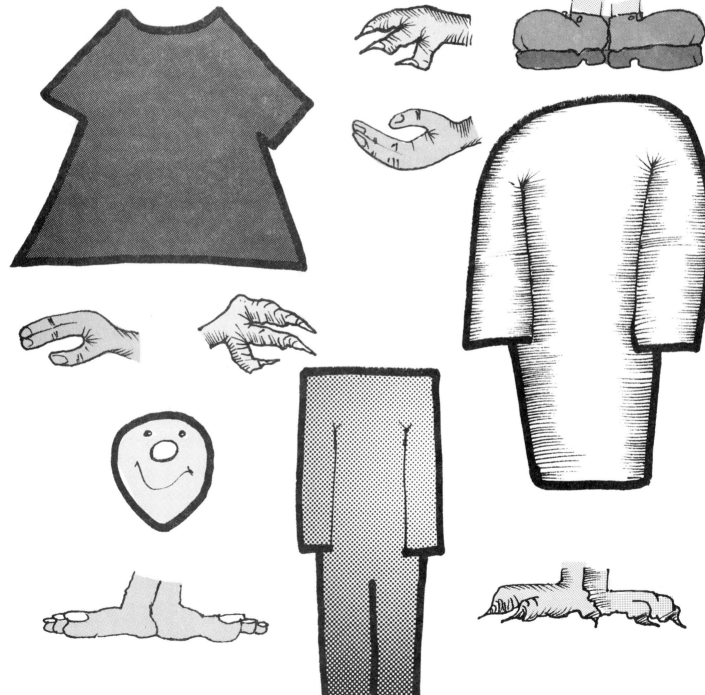

36

The Creature

Creative Thinking Skills   Visualization (construction) and elaboration (writing)

Getting Started

1. Encourage students to cut all pieces and then experiment with various designs before deciding on a final creation.

2. Have students use their creations as a stimulant for writing a brief story about "The Creature Who Couldn't Be Cruel!"

Afterwards   Post the stories next to the illustrations on a classroom wall.

More   Discuss the importance of separating appearance from reality. What animal species are endangered by appearances and reputations? (sharks, spiders, tigers, wolves, etc.)

Unicorns can imagine what's inside of all things.

    GA1404

Begin a Story!

Select a sentence from section 1. Do the same for sections 2 and 3. Use the three sentences as a beginning for the first paragraph of a story. Finish the beginning paragraph and then add more paragraphs until the story is finished. In section 3, the four dots mean that you should finish the sentence.

1

- On a wintry and wind howling night, the door flew open and it appeared.
- In the forest clearing, a small figure danced in the moonlight.
- The alien creature appeared from the glowing orb.
- The injured and frightened fawn stared at me from its hiding place.
- The face was wrinkled more from merriment and laughter than from age.

2

- I was stunned by the sudden realization of it all.
- Although nervous, I made an attempt to calm myself.
- I couldn't believe what I saw!
- I wanted to speak, but words failed me.
- At that moment, I questioned my wisdom for being here.

3

- And then a strange thing happened.
- To my amazement, I saw . . . .
- I hesitated and then . . . .
- My eyes searched for . . . .
- I started to . . . .

Share your story with someone else.
Get some reactions. Consider some changes in your story.
Improve it!
Read it to others.

Begin a Story!

Creative Thinking Skills   Elaboration

This exercise deals with beginning a story through a morphological synthesis strategy.

Getting Started

1. Have students select one sentence or statement from each section. For example, *"On a wintry and wind howling night, the door flew open and it appeared. I wanted to speak, but words failed me. My eyes searched for . . . ."*

2. Encourage students to finish the beginning paragraph and then add others to complete the story.

Afterwards

1. Have each student share his written story with another classmate.

2. Have each student receive reactions on the story from that classmate.

3. Provide time for designed changes in the story.

4. Have students read their stories in small groups.

Unicorns prefer learning by doing.

Which?

Select one answer from a choice of three and give a reason why.

Which gets more lumps?

☐ a misdialed telephone number

☐ a bowl of sugar

☐ a toad

Why? _____

_____

_____

_____

Which is lighter?

☐ a feather

☐ a smile

☐ autumn

Why? _____

_____

_____

_____

𝔚hich?

Creative Thinking Skills   Flexibility and elaboration

This direct analogy exercise can promote interesting and alternative insights.

Getting Started

1. Distribute copies of the exercise and indicate to students there are no wrong answers, just some interesting explanations.

2. Allow ten minutes or so for completion.

There are many possibilities to this exercise and here are a few examples with different perspectives.

- A misdialed telephone number gets some angry lumps if the person answering the phone was awakened from a sound sleep.
- Sugar gets lumpy with moisture.
- A toad has a wart-like and lumpy texture to its skin. It also swallows a lot of fat flies and that would make anything lumpy.

- A feather can float to the ground and that's light!
- A smile can ease a lot of heavy and emotional burdens.
- Tree leaves begin to fall during autumn and that makes trees a lot lighter.

Afterwards

1. Provide time for explanations.

2. Discuss the importance of viewing things from different perspectives or from a flexible perspective.

- What are the advantages?
- What are the disadvantages?

                                                                 GA1404

How Many Different Ways Could You Determine the Number of Feet on a Fast-Moving Bug?

Use some fast speed film.

_____

_____

_____

Put some used bubble gum in his path and count his legs while he's stuck.

_____

_____

_____

_____

_____

_____

_____

_____

How Many Different Ways Could You Determine the Number of Feet on a Fast-Moving Bug?

Creative Thinking Skill   Flexibility

Getting Started   This exercise in flexible thinking is for stimulating different categorical approaches to the problem. Some responses may include paint, mud or some other substance that would cause footprints, other responses may include photography or video approaches, some may include magnifying devices, some may include capture or substances that would cause the bug to slow down for a quick count and some may include studying insect classifications to determine the number of feet. The important thing is the different categories of thought as opposed to repetition of the same category, for example, footprints from paint, footprints from ink, footprints from mud, etc.

1. Use the exercise with small teams of students or administer it individually.

2. As a class, categorize the written responses to demonstrate the flexibility of thinking principle.

Afterwards   Discuss the importance of using different approaches to problem solving.

Add a Caption!

Think of some funny captions that would fit the drawing. Select your funniest; then write it on the lines below.

_____

_____

_____

_____

44

Add a Caption!

Creative Thinking Skill   Elaboration and originality

The objective is to create a humorous caption for the cartoon. Humor is likely to generate an original statement or a statement not repeated within a group of people or a class of students.

Look for a wide range of possibilities like... *Once upon a time there were three persons, a daddy person, a momma person and a little baby person,* or *"Why do earthlings look so weird, Mom?* etc.

Getting Started

1. Encourage individual students to think of two or three possibilities before selecting their funniest.

2. Share captions.

More

1. What purposes do captions serve? (humor, satire, insight, a political statement, a philosophical statement, advertising or commercial, etc.)

2. What different kinds of things might have a caption? (comic cartoons, political cartoons, photographs, works of art, such as, collages, sculpture, paintings, illustrations, T-shirts, bumper stickers, etc.)

3. Examine a newspaper. How many different kinds of captions were represented?

GA1404

Turn a Whatisit into a Thisisit!

Look at this!
Look at it upside down!
Turn it into something rightside up or upside down.

Think about it!
Draw it!
Share it!
Talk about it!

46

Turn a Whatisit into a Thisisit!

Creative Thinking Skill   Visualization, transformations and elaboration

Transformations deal with **making changes with or on an existing concept**. In this exercise the changes include combining, adding, adapting, modifying and, perhaps rearranging.

Getting Started   Distribute copies of the exercise, and have students visualize what it could be turned into. They may turn it upside down and complete the image or complete the image as it appears.

Afterwards   Encourage students to talk about their completed image.

• What is it?
• How does it function?
• What unique qualities does it have?

More   Write or tell a story about a day in the life of THISISIT!

Unicorns are only seen by true believers!

GA1404

List Things You Can't Touch!

love
_____

Check (√) the seven most important!

List Things You Can't Touch!

Creative Thinking Skill   Fluency

The purpose of this activity is to stimulate thinking in part, towards abstract concepts, for example, love, happiness, honesty, justice, freedom, cooperation, caring, democracy, etc. This will provide an opportunity to view and explore the importance of abstract or difficult-to-define concepts within our lives.

Getting Started

1. Either use as an individual activity or within teams of two or three students.

2. Provide ten minutes for completion.

Afterwards

Share the seven most important concepts listed on each exercise sheet. Provide time for a justification of the most important concepts cited.
- In what ways are they important?
- How would our lives be different without them?
- Why are these words difficult to define?

More

Challenge students to write a definition for the word *justice*. Compare results and determine how many students wrote a similar definition.

Draw and Describe a Noun

- Anything that can be drawn is a noun.
- Draw a noun in the box.
- Write some describing words or adjectives that would describe your drawn noun outside the box.
- Search in the dictionary to find a few unique describing words.

offensive
strange
odoriferous
ugly
obtrusive

unglamorous

50

GA1404

Draw and Describe a Noun

Creative Thinking Skills   Visualization and elaboration

Getting Started   Encourage students to draw an object or thing within the box. Then encourage dictionary use to find adjectives that would best describe the object or thing drawn. For a quick assessment on words selected, have students examine their words in association with the object or thing drawn, for instance, an *offensive* foot, a *strange* foot, an *odoriferous* foot, an *ugly* foot, an *obtrusive* foot, an *unglamorous* foot. The italicized words describe the noun *foot* and adjectives describe nouns.

Afterwards   Share noun drawings and adjectives.

More   Add an appropriate adverb to each adjective. For example: A *very* offensive foot, an *incredibly* strange foot, etc.

Unicorns are forever!

GA1404

Hats for Ats

Ats are armless four-legged creatures who are bothered by troublesome gnats.

- Brainstorm as many different kinds of hats as you can. Write them on the lines below.

- Then select five hats that would best suit Ats. Draw your five selected hats on the five Ats.

- Explain why your five selected and drawn hats are best for Ats.

stocking cap _____   _____   _____

_____   _____   _____

_____   _____   a Viking's helmet _____

_____   _____   _____

_____   _____   _____

_____   _____   _____

Hats for Ats

Creative Thinking Skills   Fluency, flexibility, elaboration and visualization

This exercise is a variation of an exercise in *I Believe in Unicorns* (Stanish, 1979). It is also an exercise in utilizing a criterion in selecting five promising solutions from a list of potential solutions or in other words, an important step in effective problem solving.

Getting Started

1. Encourage students to visualize different kinds of vocations, recreational or athletic events and fashionable or informal events and costumes worn at costume parties. Have them visualize the kind of hats worn in these jobs or at these events.

2. Have them list the hats they visualized on the exercise sheet. For example, a hockey helmet, a hard hat, a cowboy hat, a policeman's hat, a high fashion hat, etc.

3. Select five different hats from the list for the five Ats. Draw the hats on the Ats and then provide a spoken justification for the hats. The hats are to assist Ats from bothersome gnats. The five chosen should be the most effective hats for doing this.

Afterwards   Share and laugh about it!

         GA1404

List Different Advantages of Having a Lizard in Your Coat Pocket!

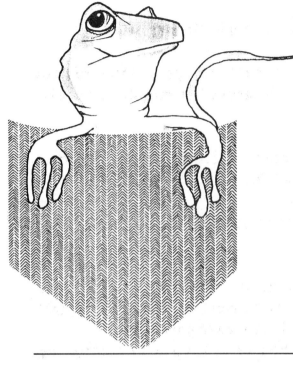

Scare away moths! _____

_____

_____

_____

_____

_____

_____

_____

_____

_____

_____

_____

_____

_____

_____

_____

_____

_____

_____

_____

_____

_____

List Different Advantages of Having a Lizard in Your Coat Pocket!

Creative Thinking Skills　　Fluency, flexibility and originality

Getting Started　　Place your class in small groups of three to four students and provide about ten minutes of brainstorming time.

Afterwards

1. Determine the group which had more responses not duplicated in other groups (originality).

2. Determine the group with the most responses (fluency).

3. Determine the group which had a response distribution across different categories of thought (flexibility). To do this, have groups place...

   an x by all responses dealing with controlling insects

   an o by all responses dealing with color

   a Δ by all responses dealing with frightening others

   a √ by all responses dealing with having a pet

   a • by all responses dealing with a function. For example, stirring soup with its tail, turning book pages, etc.

More　　Write a humorous story about a lazy lizard named Lizzy who lived in Linda's lovely lavender linen coat pocket.

GA1404

Enumerable

See how many different mathematical statements you can write in a seven-minute time period using numbers from each of the three columns. Use any mathematical operation you desire as long as the statement is correct. Follow the column sequence; that is, use a number from Column 1 first, a number from Column 2 second and a number from Column 3 last to construct correct statements. One selection from each column must be used for all statements.

Example: $32 \div 4 = 8$

Column 1	Column 2	Column 3
32	2	72
33	3	11
3	4	16
44	16	3
8	9	24
12	11	17
4	5	8

GA1404

Enumerable

Creative Thinking Skills   Fluency and flexibility

This exercise features two elements of creative productivity. Using a matrix or columns for generating various and multiple outcomes or ideas is a strategy called morphological synthesis. The other element is breaking the threshold of habit-bound thinking. There will be some students who will discover that creating a mathematical operation between double-digit numbers can generate even more statements. For example, in Column 1, a number such as 33 may be written 3 + 3 and used with other numbers in Columns 2 and 3 to create a statement.

Getting Started   Tell students they can add, subtract, multiply or divide. The objective is to create as many correct statements as possible within a seven-minute time period.

Afterwards   1. Determine who had the most statements.

2. Determine how many different accurate statements were generated by the class as a group.

More   Encourage a committee of students to develop more matrixes and numbers for classroom use.

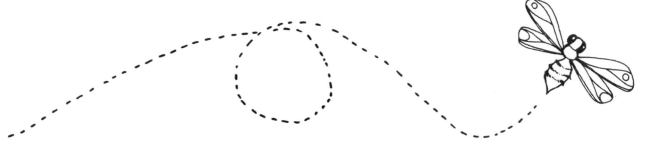

GA1404

$\mathfrak{D}$raw a Wish!

• Think about a wish!
• Draw the wish by using the drawn *W* as a part of it!
• Explain why your wish is important.

My wish is important because _____

_____

_____

_____

_____

GA1404

Draw a Wish!

Creative Thinking Skills   Visualization and elaboration

Getting Started

1. Provide two minutes of quiet individual thinking time on personal wishes.

2. Challenge students to use the drawn *W* on the exercise page within their drawing of a personal wish. Encourage embellishment of the drawing with lines, colored markers, crayons or other media.

3. Encourage students to explain in writing why their wishes are important.

Afterwards   Share drawings and explanations.

More   Discuss the importance of wishing to goal set.

Unicorns favor those who try.

GA1404

Name an Invention and Give It Some Functions

Give this invention a name and provide it with a function or functions. Select an operation or two or three from among the four columns of words. Use your selected words in helping you describe how the invention functions.

Operations

powderizes	records	rolls	separates
zip or zap	spins	deflates	dissolves
projects	speaks	chews	flattens
presses	reads	wraps	bags
heats	disposes	squeezes	announces

Description

_____

_____

_____

_____

_____

_____

_____

_____

_____

_____

_____

_____

_____

_____

Invention's name: _____

GA1404

Name an Invention and Give It Some Functions

Creative Thinking Skills   Visualization and elaboration

Visualization is involved here because the illustration stimulates ideation. Elaboration is accommodated for detailing and describing the invention's functions and purposes.

Getting Started   Provide the exercise sheet to all students. Encourage students to name the invention last. In other words, determine and write about how the invention functions as a preliminary step before naming it.

An example:

Description

This postal invention receives a letter or package, and when the lever is pushed down it electronically **reads** the address and then stamps a **ZIP** code on it. At the same time the speaker **announces** through its speaker system the ZIP code for the customer's information and convenience.

Invention's name: The Postal Zipper

Note: The boldfaced words are words selected from Operations on the student exercise page.

Afterwards   Share student responses in class.

Draw in a Habitat for This!

Add a habitat or an environment to this picture.

Gather some clues from your picture and tell a story about the creature. Tell about where and how it lives and survives.

Draw in a Habitat for This!

Creative Thinking Skills   Elaboration and visualization

Look for enrichment, embellishment and elaboration of detail in student drawings.

Getting Started

1. List, as a class, different habitats or environments, for example, ponds, lakes, rivers, bayous, oceans, grasslands, swamps, tropical rain forests, deserts, mountains, plateaus, plains, tundras, etc.

2. Encourage students to select a habitat and draw elements of it within the frame of the picture. This will add to the clues within the picture. For example, if the environment is a desert, then cacti and a hot sun could be added. The creature's long toes might suggest burrowing into the desert soil for protection from the sun or for penetrating cacti for water. Challenge students to associate the creature's attributes with the habitat they chose.

3. Using the information added to the picture along with the original illustration of the creature, students are to tell a story about it.

Afterwards

Cite examples of how the attributes of any animal are associated with its habitat. For example, the claws of a bear are used for capturing fish in nearby streams; the fur is important to hibernation in winter, etc.

63

GA1404

How Many Different Uses for a Pen?

Think conventional! Think conventional!

Use as a birdhouse perch.

_____

_____

_____

Use the beginning three letters to spell _Pennsylvania_.

_____

_____

_____

Use it to stir a magic formula.

_____

_____

_____

_____

_____

_____

_____

_____

_____

_____

_____

_____

GA1404

How Many Different Uses for a Pen?

Creative Thinking Skills   Fluency, flexibility and originality

Use this activity as a warm-up for a discussion on any subject.

Getting Started   The three examples contain three different categories of thought, for example, a replacement concept, a semantic concept and a stirring concept. Using different categories of thought is a creative factor of thinking generally referred to as flexibility. Make sure that in some fashion the examples are provided or presented to students before they begin the exercise.

Provide five minutes for completion.

Afterwards
1. Share responses.
2. Acknowledge the one-of-a-kind response (originality).

Unicorns come in all colors, shapes and sizes.

My Mother's Purse

Imagine that things in your mother's purse could wonder about things. What do you suppose they would wonder about? Think of four things that would likely be in your mother's purse. List the four things on the lines provided; then write some *wondering* dialogue for them.

1. _____   3. _____

2. _____   4. _____

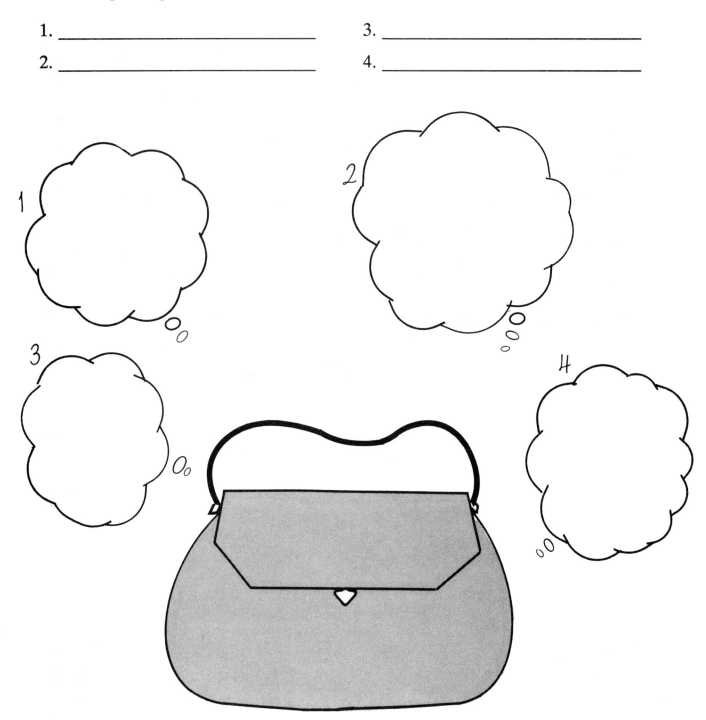

My Mother's Purse

Creative Thinking Skills   Visualization and elaboration

Getting Started

1. Distribute copies of the exercise and have each student imagine at least ten things that might be in his mother's purse.

2. Encourage students to select four items that might have something to wonder about. For example, one shade of lipstick might question the beauty of another… "That lipstick shade clashes with everything she's wearing!"

3. Challenge students to use quotation marks correctly and to provide humor whenever possible.

Afterwards   Share written responses.

More

Try some of these questions.
- Which item in your mother's purse is frequently lost?
- Which item has been in your mother's purse the longest?
- Which item in your mother's purse is the most difficult to find?
- Which item in your mother's purse would be the most argumentative? Why?

GA1404

⏺rite a Tale

Select any combination of items from each of the four groups and then add a happy ending for a written tale. For example, one could write a tale about a baby unicorn held in a dungeon by a bad-tempered sorcerer who intends to feed it poison.

1. Protagonist (Hero)
   - a baby unicorn
   - the good elf
   - a beautiful princess
   - a handsome prince
   - a lost traveler
   - a knight in armor
   - the good magician
   - you

2. Setting
   - a forest clearing
   - a castle
   - mountain ledge
   - a dungeon
   - a cave
   - a forsaken dwelling
   - in a deep pit
   - in a chamber of horrors

3. Antagonist (Villain)
   - a wicked witch
   - an ogre
   - an evil wizard
   - Wicked Willie
   - a giant Titan
   - a gremlin
   - a bad-tempered sorcerer
   - a creature from the dark lagoon

4. Problem (Conflict)
   - tied up
   - to be fed to a dragon
   - being held for ransom
   - given an evil spell
   - about to be tortured
   - about to be poisoned
   - held hostage forevermore
   - about to be torched by fire

GA1404

Write a Tale

Creative Thinking Skills   Elaboration

This exercise nurtures elaboration of thought through morphological synthesis. Morphological synthesis utilizes word groups or matrixes to generate ideas.

Getting Started   1. Explain to students how the four groups can generate a story theme for writing purposes. For example, ask a student to select a protagonist from group 1. Ask another student to select a setting from group 2. Ask still another student to select an antagonist from group 3 and a fourth student to select a problem from group 4.

2. Summarize the four selections into a synthesis. For example, a beautiful princess is in a deep pit. She was placed there by a bad-tempered sorcerer who wants to feed her to a dragon. Explain to students that each story must have a happy ending so the problem or conflict must be resolved. For example, the princess might free herself by outwitting both the dragon and the sorcerer through her own cleverness of thought.

Afterwards   Share the various stories in class.

Unicorns are color-blind and they see value in being so.

    GA1404

Curve Drawings

Turn each pair of curves into a drawing. Each drawing must be a different topic.

Example:

Curve Drawings

Creative Thinking Skills　Flexibility, visualization and transformations

This exercise can be a stimulator for viewing and appreciating varying points of view or different perspectives.

Getting Started　Provide five to ten minutes for completion.

Afterwards

1. Determine how many different subjects or topics were drawn.

2. Promote a discussion by asking…
   "How many different opinions or points of view do you suppose there are on television programming?" Name a few! (too violent, entertaining, not challenging, a waste of time, educational, etc.)

   • Which is correct?

   • What factors influence opinions on issues such as television programming?

   • Why is it important to have different opinions, points of view or perspectives on a given subject?

   • In what ways was the exercise on curve drawings like television programming?

More　List other issues in which there are many and varied points of view.

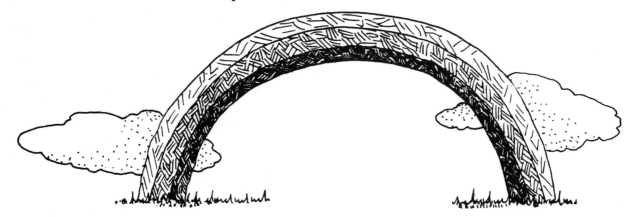

How Might You Safely Get an Alligator out of a Supermarket?

Lasso him.

Lure him out with "Gatorade."

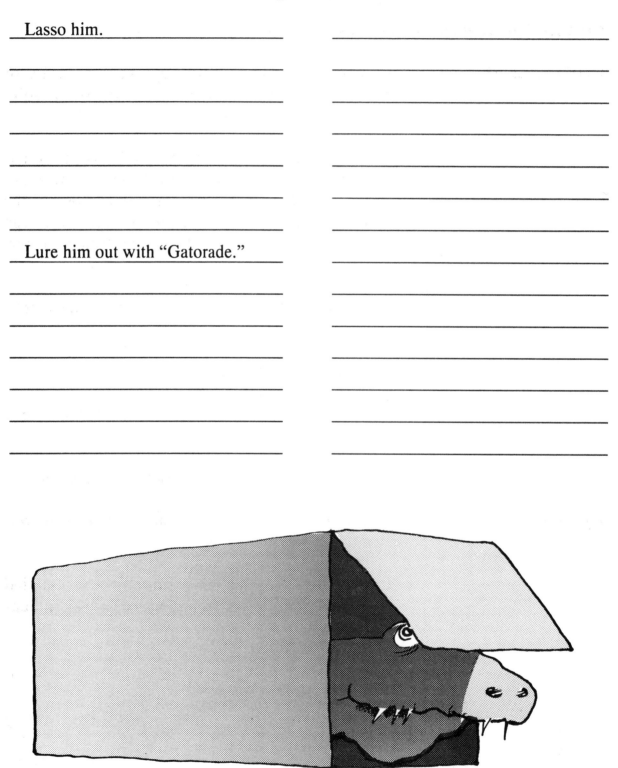

How Might You Safely Get an Alligator out of a Supermarket?

Creative Thinking Skills   Fluency and originality

Getting Started   This activity promotes fluency and originality of thought and some of the skills of group problem solving.

1. Place your class in small groups of five to six students. Encourage each group to select a recorder for ideas. Provide the recorder with a copy of the activity page for recording group ideas. Encourage the recorder to record all ideas regardless of how ridiculous they might appear.

2. Allow five to eight minutes of group brainstorming time.

3. Have each group select their...
   • funniest solution
   • solution they think no other group would come up with
   • most practical solution
   • solution that would be safest for the alligator

Afterwards   1. Determine the group that had the most solutions (fluency).

2. Determine the group that had more one-of-a-kind solutions or solutions not repeated in other groups (originality).

73

Draw a Giraforilla and Write a Dictionary-Type Entry on It!

gi·raf·o·ril·la (jə-răf′-ō-rĭl′ə) *n.*

_____

_____

_____

_____

_____

_____

_____

74

Draw a Giraforilla and Write a DictionaryType Entry on It!

Creative Thinking Skills

Transformations, visualization, originality and elaboration

Getting Started

This exercise, in addition to addressing a few creative thinking skills, provides an opportunity to acquaint or reacquaint students with the various conventions used in a dictionary word entry.

1. Challenge students to combine, in a drawing, the attributes of a giraffe and a gorilla into a single mammal.

2. The second step in this exercise is to develop a dictionary-type entry for a giraforilla. The conventions of the entry word, the syllabication, the pronunciation and the part of speech is provided for them. The remaining conventions are for them to provide. Encourage them to study dictionary entries to gather an understanding of what is needed to make the giraforilla appear to be a living creature. Referring to dictionary entries on *giraffe* and *gorilla* along with other animals will be helpful.

Afterwards

1. Share student products.

2. Discuss the various conventions of an entry word, such as syllabication, pronunciation, part-of-speech labels, inflected forms, field labels, cross-references, order of definitions, explanatory notes, illustrative examples, variants, idioms, etymologies, synonyms, etc., or the specific conventions used in student dictionaries.

    GA1404

A Unicorn's Horn

• Within a five-minute time period, list things a unicorn might do with its horn.

• Circle a response you think no one else in your classroom had.

_____   _____

Punch elevator floor buttons   _____

_____   _____

_____   _____

_____   Plant acorns

_____   _____

_____   _____

_____   _____

GA1404

A Unicorn's Horn

Creative Thinking Skills   Fluency and originality

This exercise will also accommodate flexibility. If desired, have students categorize their responses into categories such as things that involve digging; things that involve stirring; things that involve punching, pushing or prodding; things that require holding, hanging or suspension and a category listed as "other" to include a variety of responses in which the categories mentioned do not fit. A student listing responses covering five categories may be identified as having a high degree of verbal flexibility.

Getting Started

1. Provide a five-minute time period for response writing.

2. Ask students to count their responses. Determine those students with the most responses for fluency.

3. Determine those students who had a response no one in the classroom duplicated for originality of thinking.

Afterwards

Discuss the importance of finding different uses for things as an ongoing inventive skill. Mention microchips and plastics, synthetic fibres and a variety of things.

Unicorns are timeless!

GA1404

𝔄 Shaggy and Scratchy Creature

Using different scraps of stuff, paste together a shaggy and **scratchy creature.**

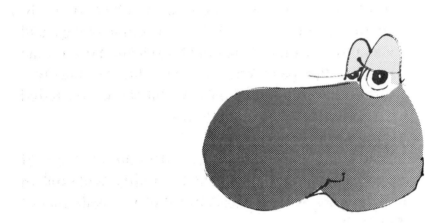

A Shaggy and Scratchy Creature

Creative Thinking Skills   Flexibility and elaboration

Getting Started

1. Encourage students to silently think of different things in a classroom that are scraps or that can be made into scraps, for example, writing paper, cardboard, construction paper, string, cloth, paper towels, rubber band pieces, newspaper scraps, broken crayons, pencil sharpener shavings, cloth, etc.

2. Students are to use glue and as many different scraps of things as needed to construct shaggy and scratchy creatures. The drawn eyes and nose on the student copy page must be incorporated in the creature's features. All the other features must be added using scraps of different things.

Afterwards

See how many students used different varieties of scraps. This would represent flexibility potential in thought along with a kinesthetic ability to elaborate or embellish.

More

For more elaboration, encourage students to describe their creatures in terms of
- Where does it live?
- What does it eat?
- What benefits would it serve?
- What kinds of unusual things does it do?

Unicorns prefer natural things.

The Happiness Tree

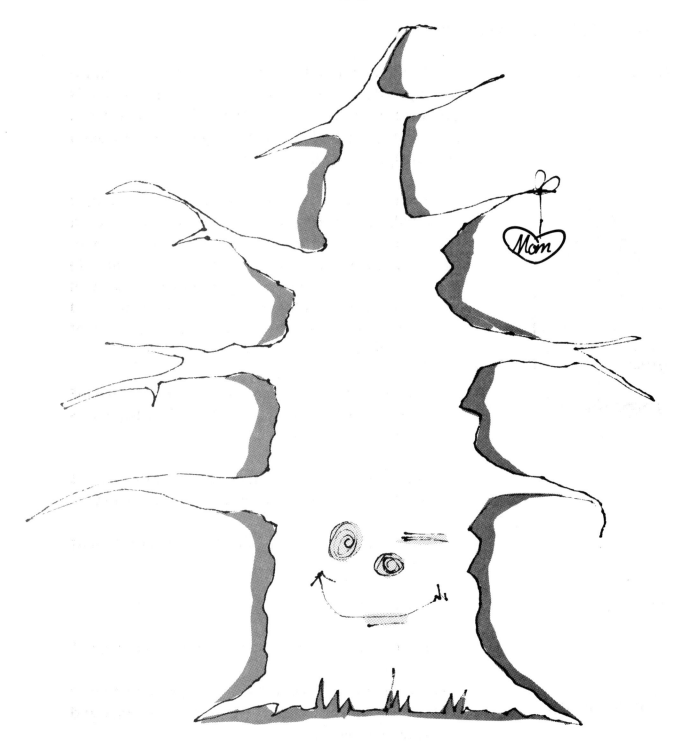

1. Think about things that make you happy!
2. Draw a lot of heartpods on the happiness tree!
3. Write your happiness things on the heartpods!
4. Compare your happiness tree with others!
5. Add some more happiness things!

80

GA1404

The Happiness Tree

Creative Thinking Skills   Fluency

Getting Started

This activity promotes some of the skills of brain-writing. After generating ideas, an opportunity is given to students to look at the ideas of others. Afterwards, more ideas will be generated through borrowing, modifying or combining.

1. Provide a copy of the activity sheet to each student and allow him to draw heartpods, and within each heartpod have him write the "happiness" item. Encourage students to think about things they do alone that make them happy; things they do with others that make them happy; certain people who make them happy; and things they see, hear or taste that make them happy.

2. After ten minutes into the activity, allow students five minutes of share time to share their happiness trees with several members of the class.

3. Have students return to their desks and add more happiness items. Give them five minutes to do this.

4. Encourage students to decorate or color their happiness trees.

Afterwards

1. Display them!

2. Discuss the importance and meaning of *happiness*!

More

Discuss the importance of "feeling happy about one's self" in solving problems, settling arguments and working on projects.

GA1404

Quacks!

Complete a few QUACKS
Who travel around
In grocery SACKS.

• Give 'em some legs!
• Give 'em some shoes!
• Give 'em some talk about being Quacks in grocery sacks.

Think of some rhyming words like the following and write a poem about Quacks in sacks: *backs, cracks, packs, racks, shacks, slacks, smacks, snacks, stacks, whacks*, etc.

Quacks!

Creative Thinking Skills   Visualization and elaboration

This exercise is an adaptation from "Quacks in Sacks" in *I Believe in Unicorns* (Stanish, 1979).

Getting Started

1. Encourage students to draw the suggested additions on the Quacks.

2. Have students imagine what a group of Quacks might talk about and then write their conversations within the talk bubbles.

3. Conclude the exercise with a clever rhyming poem about Quacks in sacks.

Afterwards

1. Talk about the similarities between the student poems and drawings and a Dr. Seuss story. What are the appealing elements within a Dr. Seuss story? What are the appealing elements within the student creations? Begin the discussion by asking, *In what ways are your poems and drawings like the poems and drawings of Dr. Seuss?*

2. Encourage students to cut out the drawings and paste them to their poems. Post poems and drawings on classroom walls.

GA1404

How Many?

How many different "verb things" could you do with an apple?

_____ it!	_____ it!	_____ it!
_____ it!	_____ it!	_____ it!
Sketch it!	_____ it!	_____ it!
_____ it!	_____ it!	_____ it!
_____ it!	_____ it!	_____ it!
_____ it!	_____ it!	_____ it!
_____ it!	_____ it!	_____ it!
_____ it!	_____ it!	_____ it!
_____ it!	_____ it!	_____ it!
_____ it!	_____ it!	_____ it!
_____ it!	_____ it!	_____ it!
_____ it!	_____ it!	_____ it!
_____ it!	Blend it!	_____ it!
_____ it!	_____ it!	_____ it!
_____ it!	_____ it!	_____ it!
_____ it!	_____ it!	_____ it!
_____ it!	_____ it!	_____ it!
_____ it!	Rotate it!	_____ it!
_____ it!	_____ it!	_____ it!

GA1404

How Many?

Creative Thinking Skills   Fluency and flexibility

It will be amazing as to how many different things can be done to or with an apple. This is a word builder for the activity suggested under "More."

Getting Started   Provide about ten minutes for completing the exercise.

There are many, many possibilities. Here are a few. Hang it, squash it, press it, cook it, suspend it, juggle it, flatten it, peel it, bag it, refrigerate it, chew it, spin it, freeze it, decorate it, cut it, cover it, throw it, roll it, compress it, store it, float it, sell it, wash it, bounce it, smash it, frame it, catch it, squeeze it, wrap it, paint it, etc.

Afterwards   Share the verbs generated.

More

1. Tell students that what they have on their exercise sheet is an action word bank. From their word banks they are to use as many action words as they care to for writing and delivering a brief monologue entitled "My Life as a Red Apple."

2. Place students in small groups for their monologue deliveries.

GA1404

Humpback Whales and Other Things

See how many different words you can create from the letters in HUMPBACK
WHALES. Write them all around the whale.

GA1404